D0132596

TIPS FOR MEANIES

TIPS *for* MEANIES

JANE THYNNE

Illustrated by Martin Honeysett

◨ SQUARE PEG

Published by Square Peg 2014

2 4 6 8 10 9 7 5 3 1

Copyright © Jane Thynne
Illustrations © Martin Honeysett
Typeset & designed by Anna Green

First published in Great Britain in 2014 by
Square Peg, 20 Vauxhall Bridge Road, London SW1V 2SA

 Penguin
Random House
UK

www.penguinrandomhouse.com

A CIP catalogue record for this book
is available from the British Library

ISBN 9780224096034

MIX
Paper from
responsible sources
FSC® C008047

Printed and bound in China by C&C Offset Printing Co., Ltd

CONTENTS

INTRODUCTION

A while ago, in the throes of the recession, I was having a 'credit crunch lunch' with Richard Ingrams, editor of *The Oldie*, and discussing reports that the Girl Guides were to revamp their Thrift badge as a life-skill. The re-discovery of Thrift by a younger generation was welcome, Richard agreed, but perhaps parents and even grandparents might benefit from rediscovering a way of thinking that once came as second nature. So *Tips For Meanies* was born.

Thrift is the virtue of our time, the answer to meaningless conspicuous consumption, instant obsolescence and bankers' bonuses. It is Everyman's way to help both the planet and our pockets. For many people, judging by the letters I have received, thrift is more than a virtue, it is a positive passion. A thrifty mindset is about far more than saving pieces of string or finding new uses for old teabags – valuable though those tricks may be. Thrift involves lateral thinking, ingenuity, and a determination to think outside the box (as a Meanie would never say). It exercises the imagination and helps us all steal a march on those who would raid our pockets for easy profit.

Most importantly, the truly thrifty are always on the lookout for ways to add to their stock of knowledge. Hence this little book. You may not get a badge for it, but it will save you money and even better, you might have fun in the process.

MIRACLE
PRODUCTS
for
MEANIES

VINEGAR

OF ALL MIRACLE MULTI-TASKERS THAT A MEANIE SHOULD POSSESS, THE MOST VENERABLE MUST BE VINEGAR.

The ancient Romans used it as an antiseptic, it removes stains like sweat, fruit, jam, cola and mustard, it cleans coffee and tea stains from china, disinfects wooden chopping boards, and mixed with salt will clean copper, bronze and brass.

Kitchen towels soaked in vinegar will remove limescale from taps, and a cup of vinegar in a gallon of tap water will release iron in the soil for acid-loving plants like rhododendrons and azaleas.

WD40

Of the many products a Meanie should have in their arsenal, WD40 is a staple. Standing for Water Displacement at the 40th try, because it took that long to get the formula right, the product claims to have 2,000 uses, of which the more esoteric include keeping pigeons away from balconies (they hate the smell, apparently). Also try it for protecting silver from tarnishing, loosening zips, cleaning stainless steel, removing tomato stains, untangling jewellery chains, lubricating bicycles and polishing slate on fireplace surrounds.

COKE

Many eminent Meanies enjoy Coca Cola, but who knew it was also a miracle product around the home? A can of Coke emptied into the wash with detergent is a seriously good grease remover. Just run through a normal cycle and the carbonic and phosphoric acid will dissolve stains and deodorise clothes. It's also a rust-buster. You can clean a blackened saucepan by simmering Coke in it, and loosen a rusty bolt or lock with just a few drops.

SILICA AND SANDWICH BAGS

Meanies who would like to spend less time polishing silver should try storing it in a sealed plastic sandwich bag. Placing a piece of ordinary blackboard chalk in your silver-drawer or jewellery chest also makes it tarnish slower. Because silver tarnishes more quickly in humid conditions, save the small sachets of silica that come in new bags and shoes, and put them wherever your silver is kept.

EVEN IN SUMMER, THERE
IS MANY A DAMP AND
HUMID AREA LURKING
IN A MEANIE'S HOME.
RATHER THAN SHELL
OUT ON AN ELECTRIC
DEHUMIDIFIER, YOU CAN
MAKE YOUR OWN FROM
CHARCOAL BARBECUE
BRIQUETTES. PLACED
IN A LARGE CAN WITH
HOLES IN THE LID,
THE BRIQUETTES WILL
READILY ABSORB NEARBY
DAMP AND ODOURS.
AFTER A FEW MONTHS
THEY CAN BE REPLACED
AND REUSED IN
THE BARBECUE.

...IT'S GREEN, AND IT'S MEAN!

CANDLES

Meanies ferret out festive supplies of candles at Christmas. Yet a candle possesses multi-tasking Meanie potential all year round. A rub with a candle is the best way to ease a sticking drawer or window sash and stroked on a hinge a candle is superb for fixing a squeaky door. A large candle can double as a pin cushion because the wax helps the needle to glide better. And the true Meanie will be sure to freeze their candles an hour before lighting. It makes them last longer and drip less.

WALLPAPER

Fashionable Meanies will know that wallpaper is now totally of the moment. Unfortunately, the really nice stuff might as well be made of rolled gold, given what it costs, and there is, inevitably, always some left over. One idea is to use this wallpaper as drawer liners. Covering the back  of shelving or bookcases with paper that complements the colour of the paint can also look chic. Or if you have access to a laminator, A4 size sections of wallpaper transform surprisingly well into table mats.

OLIVE OIL

Any Meanie who moans at the cost of olive oil will be relieved to find its uses extend far beyond the kitchen. As well as a safe and effective shining agent for stainless steel, this versatile oil makes a natural wood polish when mixed two parts to one with lemon juice.

CAT
LITTER

NOT EVERYONE IS LUCKY ENOUGH TO COHABIT WITH A CAT, SO MANY MEANIES HAVE YET TO DISCOVER THE FLEXIBLE USES OF CAT LITTER.

Yet what a multi-tasker this unassuming product can be. Odourless, yet odour-removing, cat litter is invaluable when sprinkled in a layer at the bottom of the kitchen bin. A small container of litter will remove smells in a fridge and it also works as a powerful deodorant in shoes that need attention. If faced with a large-scale liquid spill, you will find a single sack of cat litter can absorb more than a gallon of oil, paint or petrol.

FLOSS

Most Meanies know dental floss is cost effective because it stops your teeth falling out and may prevent heart attacks, but few appreciate the multi-tasking ability of this wonder product. Try it for sewing on hooks and buttons, stringing picture frames, supporting plants or mending fishing nets. Stop a dripping tap by tying one end of the floss round the tap and allowing the drip to travel down the drain. And when your ring gets stuck, wrapping dental floss tightly round the top of the finger will ease it gently off.

LOO ROLLS

This humble multi-tasker is already used by many Meanies in place of peat pots for planting seeds. Simply fill with compost, and when the seedling is planted out the roll will decompose. Or store your cables in individual rolls to keep them tangle free. Packed with shredded newspaper, loo rolls make excellent kindling logs, and if you flatten them and tape the ends, you have a stiff envelope for small mail.

The
MEANIE'S
TOILETTE

Mouthwash:

A MEANIE OF MY ACQUAINTANCE SPENT A FORTUNE ON EXPENSIVE ANTI-DANDRUFF SHAMPOOS UNTIL DISCOVERING THE THRIFTY PROPERTIES OF LISTERINE MOUTHWASH. LISTERINE CONTAINS THE ESSENTIAL OILS THYMOL, EUCALYPTOL, MENTHOL AND METHYL SALICYLATE, WHICH ARE THOUGHT TO BE EFFECTIVE AGAINST THE FUNGUS PITYROSPORUM OVALE, WHICH IS THE MAIN CAUSE OF DANDRUFF.

Sloosh a capful onto the scalp – not on broken skin – and leave for five minutes before rinsing off. Try it for a week and wear your black polo neck with abandon.

VASELINE

The latest miracle beauty product embraced by American fashion mavens may seem surprising – tiny £1 pots of Vaseline with a tint for 'rosy lips'. Should female Meanies need more convincing of its thrifty chic, they could also use Vaseline as a make-up remover, nail protector, eye highlighter, shoe and leather cleaner, and hair-styling product. Male Meanies, however, will find it works well to prevent corrosion on the battery terminals of the car.

OLIVE OIL

A drop of olive oil makes a brilliant make-up remover, and male Meanies will find it provides a close and moisturising shave.

SHOWER CAPS

Few Meanies will baulk at removing the odd bar of soap or complimentary shampoo bottle from their hotel. After all, these items carry the hotel's logo, so it's a bit of a branding exercise. Yet an equally useful nick can be the unattractive plastic shower cap. These make brilliant containers for storing shoes in a suitcase when travelling, to prevent them shedding dirt onto clothes.

They also work for covering bowls in the fridge, bowls of dough left to rise, and for shielding bicycle seats on rainy days.

TOOTHPASTE

Prince Charles, one of our most celebrated Meanies, acquired that reputation through his thrift with the toothpaste tube. Yet is he aware of the many 'off-brush' uses toothpaste can serve? Rubbing a blob of toothpaste onto hands after cutting onions or garlic removes smells. It cleans crayon from walls, and scuff marks from white trainers. A coat of toothpaste applied to and then wiped off swimming goggles or mirrors prevents fogging. And if your toothpaste falls in the sink, a quick rub round the taps will make chrome gleam.

SHAMPOO

Balding Meanies who are dismayed to find bottles of surplus shampoo clogging up their shelves will be relieved to find that shampoo is a multi-tasker. It's a cheap and effective replacement in liquid soap dispensers. It can work better than detergent at removing stains and is ideal for washing delicates. Mixed with conditioner it will fix a squeaky hinge and loosen bolts and zips. Combine it with baking soda to polish metal surfaces to a satisfying shine and rub it round the edges of a plaster to soften the glue and allow pain-free removal.

BATH OIL

There are all sorts of expensive ways to perfume yourself and your environment, but Meanies know it is just as effective to make your own bath oil by putting a few drops of your favourite perfume in a bottle of baby oil. When it comes to rooms, a fabric-softener sheet in a drawer or behind a chair will impart an invigoratingly clean smell. These sheets are also a great deodoriser for shoes.

FABRIC SOFTENER

RING RESCUE

SOMETIMES, THROUGH AGE OR ACCIDENT, THE RING THAT LOOKED SO LOVELY ON YOUR SLENDER PAW BECOMES WEDGED IMMUTABLY ON A SWOLLEN FINGER.

Before allowing experts to cut the ring off, try this Meanie technique. Take a length of elastic and wrap the finger from the nail downwards towards the ring, compressing the tissues. When the elastic reaches the ring, poke the end under the ring with tweezers, then rotate the elastic backwards in a spiral movement drawing the ring up the finger. The result – a rapid ring rescue!

GREASE-BUSTERS

Some Meanies feel grease stains are merely the price of a life well lived. Others prefer to keep up appearances, but without the expense of dry cleaning. If a silk garment gets in the way of your dinner, try spraying the grease stain with a good squirt of hairspray. Then rinse in a little cold water with detergent. An ingredient in the propellant of hair spray opens the pores of the fabric and voilà! the stain is released. Works well on ink stains too.

We're questioning everything these days, so let's
include washing-powder instructions. Unless your
clothes are very dirty, half the recommended amount of
powder does just as well and a teaspoon of bicarbonate
of soda acts as a whitening agent. Clothes last longer
and fade less if you wash and dry them inside out. You
will find if you halve the detergent in the dishwasher
too, your plates will emerge just as clean.

STEAM CLEAN

MANY MEANIES FIND THAT THEIR SCARVES AND TIES WILL LAST A LIFETIME, GIVEN TENDER CARE AND A RESOLUTE INDIFFERENCE TO FASHION.

Yet how to prevent them becoming crunched up at the bottom of the drawer? Even the best dressed Meanie could become better groomed with this ingenious tip: collect around ten old shower or curtain rings and slide them onto a sturdy coat hanger – this makes a compact and efficient storage space for ties and scarves and prevents them from getting creased.

The
MEANIE'S
MEDICINE
CABINET

Confectionery Cures:

MEANIES EVERYWHERE ARE DOGGED BY COUGHS AND COLDS. BUT BEFORE SPLASHING OUT IN THE CHEMIST, TRY A REMEDY CLOSER TO HAND. STUDIES SHOW THAT ONE OF THE FOREMOST INGREDIENTS IN DARK CHOCOLATE, THEOBROMINE, IS ACTUALLY MORE EFFECTIVE THAN MANY STANDARD DRUG TREATMENTS FOR A PERSISTENT COUGH, BECAUSE OF ITS IMPRESSIVE ACTION ON THE SENSORY ENDINGS OF THE VAGUS NERVE WHICH CONTROLS THE COUGH REFLEX.

Another confectionery cure is marshmallow. Extracts of the marshmallow plant, *Althaea officinalis*, have been used since ancient Egyptian times for inflamed throat membranes, and the gelatin in the modern product also relieves sore throats and soothes pain.

ASPIRIN

One of the most versatile weapons in a Meanie's armoury. Not just for headaches but for your skin. Rub it on a mosquito bite and it will soothe the itch because of its anti-inflammatory properties. Its basic ingredient, salicylic acid, appears in most athletes' foot medication as an anti-fungal. It is also the active ingredient in most anti-dandruff shampoos, so adding an aspirin to your shampoo will control scalp problems. A couple of crushed aspirins mixed with water make an effective facial mask – many skin creams contain exactly the same chemical.

MARIGOLD FLOWERS

These can be rubbed on bee stings and insect bites, having antibiotic properties.

SALT WATER

This meanie tip comes courtesy of my lovely dental hygienist, Linda, who despite being furnished with large amounts of freebie mouthwash insists that she knows better. Following scares that traditional mouthwash might variously kill useful bacteria, increase blood pressure and contain alcohol, she recommends trying a very dilute solution of humble table salt. Salt water treats gingivitis and is a natural disinfectant. It has been used as mouthwash by numerous cultures around the world. Just rinse and spit, as they say.

Tissues:

BOXED TISSUES ARE
SCARCELY A CRIPPLING ITEM
IN THE MEANIE HOUSEHOLD
BUDGET, YET THERE IS
A SAVING WHICH CAN
PROVIDE A REGULAR THRILL
OF THRIFT. FIT A LOO ROLL
INTO A CYLINDRICAL STEEL
UTENSILS HOLDER AND
REMOVE THE CARDBOARD
CORE. PULL UP THE ROLL
FROM THE MIDDLE LIKE
A TISSUE, AND TEAR OFF
WHEN REQUIRED. IT'S
CHEAP, CHIC AND MAY
PROVE CONVENIENT IF THIS
SEASON'S CHEERFULLY-
NAMED 'KILLER FLU'
ACTUALLY ARRIVES.

SOOTHING SOCKS

A CRICKED NECK CAN MAKE ANY MEANIE MISANTHROPIC, BUT DON'T RESORT TO EXPENSIVE HIGH-TECH HEATING PADS WHEN IT'S SO EASY TO MAKE YOUR OWN.

Pour several ounces of rice into an old sock and tie a knot at the end. Enclose that sock in the other sock of the pair with the tied end first, then heat the sock pad for between two and three minutes in the microwave. Position the sock pad on the neck, position yourself on the sofa, lie back and relax.

The
MEANIE
IN THE
KITCHEN
...and IN THE
GARDEN

THE 'BEST BEFORE' DATE IS THE BANE OF THE MEANIE'S LIFE. UNLIKE 'USE BY' DATES, WHICH SIGNAL POTENTIAL TOXINS, THE WEASELLY LITTLE BEST BEFORE STAMP STIGMATISES FOOD WHICH IS STILL PERFECTLY SAFE TO EAT, RESULTING IN FIVE MILLION TONS OF GOOD FOOD BEING THROWN OUT EACH YEAR. FRUGAL MEANIES HAVE LONG EMPLOYED THEIR OWN TECHNOLOGY – I.E. THEIR NOSES AND EYES – TO DETECT IF SOMETHING IS UNSAFE.

Tinned food lasts forever, unless damaged or rusty, milk won't hurt you because it's pasteurised. Learn to ignore 'Best Before'.

Just because an egg is past its 'best-before' date, doesn't make it off. Place the egg in a jug of water and watch. Fresh ones sink to the bottom and lie on their sides, while week-old eggs sink and bob slightly. Only the egg that floats is actually bad because the air pocket inside has expanded as moisture is lost.

When life gives you lemons, some people just make lemonade, but Meanies go that bit further. First maximise the juice by rolling the lemon with light pressure beforehand to burst the insides, then cut lengthwise instead of across. Zapping a lemon briefly in the microwave also produces far more juice when it's squeezed. When you've had the juice, use the peel to clean tea and coffee marks from cups. After juicing, use the remaining lemon as a natural sanitiser to remove smells from rolling pins, bowls and cutting boards. If you go away, a cut lemon left in each room removes the fusty air on your return.

Nothing ages less gracefully than a banana. One day all plump and green, the very next day black and raddled with age spots. Yet the reason for this speedy decline lies all too close to the fruit bowl. Apples! Apples exude ethylene gas which speeds up the ripening of bananas as well as avocados, peaches, plums and pears. Meanies should keep apples refrigerated, or buy Fuji and Granny Smith varieties, which don't produce much ethylene. Use the black bananas for banana bread or freeze for curries or smoothies, and use the skin to polish shoes or fertilise roses.

SHINE-N-DINE

How often, when reaching for an onion from the vegetable drawer, do you encounter a sprouted, mouldy or pungently rotting item that belies your otherwise gleaming kitchen? The answer to getting value from your onions is in the storage. Plastic bags promote sprouting, and in the fridge onions go soft and impart their smell to other foods. Storing onions next to potatoes also accelerates spoilage. Meanies who really know their onions use old brown paper bags with holes punched in them, which allows the air to circulate and can extend an onion's life by months.

The term 'cheeseparing' is defined in the OED as 'meanly economical', so it should come as no surprise that there are savings to be made in the humble world of cheese. Obviously no Meanie would buy ready-grated, but if you have an old block of cheese that has gone hard, don't chuck it; freeze it. Frozen cheese is easy to grate, and can be crumbled readily for recipes. It also pays to avoid cheese fashion. Pecorino is a cheaper choice than Parmesan, quark costs less than ricotta and Wensleydale can often substitute for feta.

HERBS

There are many virtues to supermarket shopping but buying fresh herbs is not one of them. Many Meanies flinch as they reach for the over-priced packet of dill, tarragon, coriander, or what have you, knowing that the bulk of it is doomed to wither at the back of the fridge for the next couple of weeks. The remedy is simple. Chop the unused portions of parsley, sage, basil or tarragon and freeze in ice cube trays filled with olive oil. This provides convenient-sized portions of flavoured oil for winter cooking. Voilà!

Marigold:

GARDEN SNOBS MAY RECOIL, BUT MEANIES SHOULD EMBRACE THE POT MARIGOLD, CALENDULA OFFICINALIS. A DEAD-CHEAP SUBSTITUTE FOR EXPENSIVE SAFFRON IN PAELLA AND RISOTTOS, IT PROVIDES A SIMILAR FLAVOUR AND COLOUR. JUST DRY THE PETALS IN THE MICROWAVE AND GRIND UP. IF YOU GROW THEM NEXT TO YOUR TOMATOES THEY DETER PESTS.

PASTA WATER

If you've cooked pasta, allow the water to cool and donate it to your plants. There's something about the starch and vitamins they appreciate.

For many Meanies, the solace of a nice cup of tea is offset by the pain of having to discard a perfectly good tea bag after only one use. But short of hanging up used tea bags to dry (which can spark calls to Social Services) what's the alternative? The answer is to use them on your house plants. Tea bags make good organic fertiliser, enriching the compost by raising nitrogen levels, and if you can be bothered to remove the bags, the leaves themselves can be dug in to help poor soil absorb water. Tea bags are also very handy at the bottom of plant containers to retain moisture and prevent leaks.

It's hard to imagine a more magnificent substance than coffee, which performs its priest-like task with miraculous reliability, but Meanies hoping to squeeze more value from their cup should conserve the grounds. Coffee grounds fertilise roses, azaleas, camellias and all acid-loving plants, as well as adding potassium and magnesium to compost. A sprinkle of coffee grounds repels ants, and makes a powerful deodoriser for fridge or car. And if you scatter coffee grounds over the ashes in a fireplace, it minimises dust when clearing.

GREENS

MEANIES WHO GROW THEIR
OWN VEGETABLES KNOW HOW
PAINFUL IT IS TO THROW ANY
AWAY, YET WE ALL TEND TO
CHUCK OUT VALUABLE VEG FOR
NO REASON.

Broccoli eaters should know that the oft-discarded stem contains just as much protein, calcium, iron and vitamins as the florets, but even greater levels of healthy phytochemicals.

Carrot tops have a parsley-like flavour and are good boiled up for a stock, as are celery leaves.

Cauliflower leaves are perfectly edible and taste like cabbage.

Meanies who love to cook should stick to stainless steel. Cheap non-stick pans are never value for money, needing replacing every few years, whereas stainless steel lasts more than thirty years. And non-stick fans could be risking not just their money but their health. Using metal utensils on non-stick surfaces causes the toxic coating to flake off and enter your food. The fumes they give off at very high temperatures have proved lethal to birds and can produce flu-like symptoms in humans. For that reason non-stick pans should be washed by hand, not in the dishwasher. It's altogether cheaper and easier to stick to stainless steel.

The Meanie's best friend is the freezer. But keeping a full freezer saves money too, because it costs less to keep a full freezer cold than an empty one. The same logic applies to the oven – if you fill it up with baking trays it creates a smaller space to heat, so the oven gets hot quicker.

A science lesson: when you take something out of the freezer you should put it into the refrigerator to thaw out slowly. By doing that the refrigerator is cooled by the deep-frozen food and will use less energy, whereas if left to stand in the kitchen the central heating will have to use more energy to compensate for the cold object unfreezing. Not forgetting that you're less likely to get poisoned by food that has thawed at a lower temperature. The only question remains, in certain Meanie homes, which is colder – inside the fridge, or out?

When polishing brass or copper, don't bother with specialised polishes. Rubbing with **tomato ketchup** or **brown sauce** gets brilliant results. Why pay for drain cleaner when a combination of **vinegar** and **baking soda** in a ratio of 2:1 will clear drains and keep them smelling good? And instead of buying expensive leather food, a mixture of two parts of **linseed oil** to one of **white vinegar** rubbed on leather furniture will keep it soft.

How many Meanies have looked on with dismay as their sparkling glassware turns cloudy after a few cycles in the dishwasher? Yet who wants to fork out on expensive glass-cleaners for an apparently minor travail? Luckily, a gratifyingly thrifty solution is at hand. Take a **potato skin** and rub the stained glass with the flesh side. Potato skin also works on stainless steel sinks and taps. Alternatively, rub your glass with a little **white toothpaste** and watch the residue disappear.

...is generally a pejorative, but to Meanies it's a badge of honour. Jars of mustard, garlic or ginger, for example, can seem useless when nearly empty. But pour in a little olive oil, replace the lid and shake, and you have a fresh salad dressing. A reader recommends the same trick with almost empty sauce bottles, to which he adds a spoonful of water and shakes like a cocktail waiter. A strong candidate for the Meanie Order of Thrift.

The
MEANIE
AT WORK
...and AT
LEISURE

IN THE OFFICE

PRINTER INK, AS ALL MEANIES ARE AWARE, IS MORE EXPENSIVE THAN CHAMPAGNE AND SO MUCH LESS ENJOYABLE.

Obvious savings include refilled cartridges or, if you print a lot of black and white documents, switching to a laser printer using toner. But how about the font? Thinner fonts use less ink than bold fonts like Arial Bold or Impact, and sans-serif fonts are more economical than serif fonts because no ink is wasted printing out little tails. Surveys claim the cheapest font is Century Gothic and switching from Arial to Century Gothic saves a staggering 31 per cent in printing costs.

Biros:

WHEN LASZLO BIRO
INVENTED THE FIRST
BALLPOINT IN 1938, HE
USED A THICKER KIND OF
INK THAT DRIED QUICKLY.
UNFORTUNATELY,
SOMETIMES THE INK
GETS STUCK BEFORE THE
CARTRIDGE IS FINISHED.
WHEN YOUR BALLPOINT
CLOGS UP BUT YOU CAN
STILL SEE INK, DON'T
THROW IT OUT. RUNNING
THE TIP LIGHTLY DOWN
THE RUBBER SOLE OF
A SHOE WILL MAKE THE
INK RUN AGAIN LIKE
MAGIC.

ENERGY SAVINGS

Vampires are more than just the latest teen craze. 'Vampire power' is the term used to describe the energy lost by leaving your DVD player, TV or microwave on standby, or when you use a power adapter for your laptop computer. Due to our ludicrous number of standby devices, vampire power now accounts for around 10 per cent of a household's total energy consumption. Meanies should switch off at the plug.

A dead battery tests every Meanie's credulity. How can we be sure that every drop of power has been squeezed from the thing? One way is to drop the battery from a short distance onto a hard surface. A charged battery will bounce once and fall over but empty ones bounce repeatedly. Even then, sometimes rubbing a battery will revive it because friction warms the chemicals inside, increasing the reaction rate. If you need AA batteries and only have AAA, insert one and wedge a ball of foil against the device's negative terminal for a stopgap solution.

RECYCLE

Many of you will recall the days when you got a penny for returning your lemonade bottle. But there are plenty of other things that can be recycled for rather heftier amounts of cash. Laptops, iPods, inkjet cartridges and digital cameras can all be sold, even broken ones. If you have an old mobile phone lying around it could fetch up to £400, and supermarkets like Tesco will give you vouchers. Numerous recycling centres can be found online, like **www.recyclingforcash.co.uk** who will pick up big items from your home for free and pay you a cheque within days.

OLD RAGS
OLD BONES
COMPUTERS
MOBILE PHONES

FREECYCLE

FOR MEANIES WITH COMPUTERS, THE BEST MONEY-SAVING SCHEME HAS TO BE FREECYCLE, WHICH ALLOWS YOU TO DONATE ITEMS YOU DON'T WANT, OR REQUEST ANYTHING YOU NEED.

Visit **www.freecycle.org** and you will be directed to your nearest group. I found garden sheds, church pews, hoovers, dishwashers, bikes, and office chairs on offer. There are 500 groups in Britain aimed at reducing waste and saving on landfill. Or, as someone else said, it's like eBay, but you don't have to pay…

FREEPOST

For any Meanies still corresponding by post, expensive postcards can be a headache. By using spare photographs instead you can save money and prevent a tsunami of unwanted photos tipping out whenever you open the drawer. But although this adds a delightfully personal touch to your correspondence, some discrimination is required. Dud snaps of yourself on the beach, for example, could prove not so much charming, as alarming.

CURB COLD CALLS

The price of thrift is eternal vigilance. A relaxing evening can often be ruined by cold calls from people with Geordie accents offering to sell you a financial service or a dream kitchen. To prevent dangerous spikes in blood pressure (and buying a new kitchen) register with the Telephone Preference Service. It's free and it means any British company must check your number against a list before they call, or face a £5,000 fine. Register on **www.mpsonline.org.uk/tps**.

AT THE SUPERMARKET

Treat shopping as a form of psychological warfare. Refuse to follow the supermarket route – you are guided to the most expensive and discretionary stuff like fresh fruit first, with the staples like cereal at the back and in the middle of rows. The most expensive items will be placed at eye level, so look up or down for better choices. Avoid traps to make you stop, like displays or samples, because you will buy more. Remember, shops dump items in bins to make them look like bargains, even when they're not.

Even Meanies without grandchildren should take a trip to the baby product aisle. Infant ranges are frequently better and cheaper than their grown-up equivalents. Always buy cotton wool, for example, in the baby section of Boots and use baby wipes rather than high tech ones for cleaning keyboards. Baby oil is superb for polishing steel surfaces and baby shampoo is far less expensive than specialist products for hand-washing cashmere, silk and wool.

AT THE SHOPS

All true Meanies know it is often more pleasurable not to buy something than to actually to part with the cash. The thrill of having resisted always puts a spring in the step. Take this further with a 30-day list. Note down the desired object and its price, and return in 30 days with a plan to buy. It will amaze you how much less desirable the object seems. If you have an Amazon account you should form a wish-list to this end, and see how rapidly your wishes fade. Procrastination may be the thief of time, but it's an absolute gift to the impulse buyer.

Meanies wandering into Starbucks are often taken aback by the gargantuan size of the frothing vats of coffee on offer. There are three sizes displayed on the menu board, 'tall', 'grande' and 'venti', and the smallest of these is a substantial twelve ounces. It happens, however, that the company does make a cheaper 'short' cappuccino which equates to a normal-sized cup, with just as much espresso. They will serve this to you if you ask for it, but for most of us it remains a secret because, for some curious reason, Starbucks can't find room on their menu board to display it…

AT THE RESTAURANT

Most Meanies, no matter how thrifty, will sometimes find themselves in a restaurant. That is when they need to understand 'menu science', the tricks restaurants use to get you to spend. Beware of dishes in white boxes, highlighted or with a lot of space around them, because it's those the chef wants to shift. Menu science indicates that customers tend to order items directly above and below the priciest dish, so be aware what the restaurant wants you to buy. Decode the menu and you can defeat the culinary conspiracy!

AT THE AIRPORT

Airports are rarely relaxing places, but the rip-off prices of drinks and meals to be consumed while waiting for your delayed plane can send stress levels into the stratosphere. Many Meanies get round this by booking a lounge pass, which gives you free food, drink, newspapers and TV in a civilised atmosphere for little more than a tenner. Try **www.holidayextras.co.uk** or **www.loungepass.com**.

The
ANIMAL-
LOVING
MEANIE

DOGS

WHEN IT COMES TO PETS, EVEN THE FLINTIEST MEANIE CAN MELT.

But why pay for a trip to the vet if all you need is a little advice? Animal-lovers can get 24-hour help from a vet at The Dogs' Trust, even if they have a cat or a parrot. For £10 a year the over-60s get unlimited telephone consultations from a qualified veterinary nurse, as well as third party insurance (for dogs only).

For information, see **www.dogstrust.org.uk** or write to Dogs' Trust, 17 Wakley Street, London EC1V 7RQ, or call 0207 837 0006.

Furballs:

IN SOME HOMES, A SOFA COVERED IN CAT HAIR IS DE RIGUEUR, BUT MANY MEANIES LIKE A MORE PRISTINE ENVIRONMENT. THOSE WHO CANNOT BRING THEMSELVES TO BUY HAIR-REMOVAL GADGETS SHOULD RUB SURFACES WITH A DAMP RUBBER GLOVE OR A SHEET OF FABRIC SOFTENER, WHICH BREAKS THE STATIC BOND THAT MAKES CAT OR DOG HAIR CLING.

CAT FOOD

Tough times may tempt Meanies to credit crunch the cat. But beware before switching to cheaper cat food! It's counter-intuitive, but buying an expensive brand works out cheaper in the long run and saves on vet's fees. Cheap food is bulked out with carbohydrate filler, leading to diabetes, obesity and kidney failure. Better brands contain far more protein, so the cat eats less yet absorbs more of the nutrition he needs.

...AND LITTER

Journalists are sadly familiar with the adage that today's newspapers are tomorrow's budgie-cage liners. Yet those who subscribe to newspaper home delivery services may want to explore this idea a little further. The plastic wrap in which the newspapers are delivered has exactly the same dimensions as the most popular type of cat litter tray, and once unwrapped can easily be fitted to make a perfect free liner for your mog. What's more, they're biodegradable, giving Meanies double Brownie points on the environmental front.

The
MEANIE'S
YEAR

SPRING

On the one hand, spring is good for Meanies, because longer daylight saves on electricity. On the other hand it gets harder to ignore the frills of dust that have collected between the folds of the curtains. But how to avoid a trip to the dry cleaners that will be expensive enough to induce palpitations? Try this. Take a dusty curtain, remove the hooks and place it in the tumble dryer together with a wet towel. Run for fifteen minutes and the towel will pick up the dust, leaving the curtain noticeably cleaner and brighter. Spring cleaning sorted…

SUMMER!

Picnic weather! As masochist Meanies know, this calls for blankets, padded jackets and a thermos of something piping hot. Too often, though, when you open your thermos, it smells of rotted vegetation. To avoid a stinky thermos, rinse with baking soda, then store with a teaspoon of salt inside. A clove will achieve the same results. For larger cool boxes, a charcoal briquette will work. In this way your picnic, like your weather, will remain bracingly fresh.

Aphid Attack:

IN SUMMER, THE MEANIE'S GARDEN IS FULL OF ROSES AND THE ROSES ARE FULL OF GREENFLY. BEFORE UNLEASHING CHEMICAL WARFARE, TRY SPRAYING THE PLANTS WITH WATER IN WHICH YOU HAVE BOILED LEMON, LIME AND ORANGE RIND. APHIDS ABSOLUTELY HATE CITRUS OIL. STEEPING SEVERAL CLOVES OF GARLIC IN WATER WITH A TABLESPOON OF CHILLI FLAKES IS ANOTHER FRUGAL AND ORGANIC REPLACEMENT FOR TOXIC BUG BLASTERS.

AND SO TO

AUTUMN,

SEASON OF MISTS AND...MOTHBALLS

According to Rentokil, moth infestations are steeply on the rise, due to central heating and increased insulation, which means too many meanies' clothes are fragranced with *eau de mothball*.

While it's true that moths prefer cashmere and shun synthetic material, what they most like are dirty clothes because the larva of the moth feeds on keratin, the protein found in hair, skin and nails. Organic sweat and skin residue are their bread and butter. So always wash jumpers before storing, keep them in plastic bags, and if you have to use a repellent, choose lavender or cedar. Remember, mothballs repel so much more than moths.

THE MEANIE
IN MIDWINTER

That time of year when Meanies have to choose between paying higher energy bills or sitting in a freezing draught. A third of all heat is lost through house walls. But if you're over 70, don't make the mistake of paying for cavity wall insulation. Because if you are, then courtesy of the government, it's free! Contact your energy supplier who will put you in touch with an installer and send round a surveyor. You might well find you qualify for free loft insulation too.

Pricey petrol is the bane of a Meanie's life. The good news is it's actually better to fill up in winter when the service station storage tanks are cold, because the colder the ground, the denser the petrol. Try to keep your car as full as possible to minimise the amount of air in the tank. Petrol vaporises fast and air in the tank will allow it to evaporate. Keeping tyres at the correct pressure also matters because deflated tyres increase petrol consumption.

THE MEANIE AT

CHRISTMAS

NOTHING BRINGS ON A FIT OF THRIFTINESS MORE THAN CHRISTMAS PREPARATIONS.

When dressing the tree use paperclips to hang ornaments. If you have finished with candles, collect up the stubs because they work as good replacements for firelighters. Shred any used wrapping paper for future present packing, or indeed the hamster cage. And as guests turn up the heating, remind them that a light jumper adds two degrees and a heavy one four degrees of warmth.

WHAT DO YOU GIVE THE MEANIE WHO HAS EVERYTHING? THERE COMES A TIME IN ALL OUR LIVES WHEN BUYING BIRTHDAY GIFTS TURNS FROM TREAT TO TORTURE. FORTUNATELY, IN THE AGE OF THE KINDLE, REAL BOOKS ARE INCREASINGLY COLLECTIBLE. A BARGAIN FIRST EDITION OR ATTRACTIVE RETRO VOLUME FROM A CHARITY SHOP WILL DELIGHT A MEANIE WITH A MANIA FOR HISTORY.

The Oxfam website even allows you to browse online: see **www.oxfam.org.uk/shop/books**.

JANE THYNNE

was born in Venezuela and educated in London. She graduated from Oxford University with a degree in English and joined the BBC as a journalist. She has also worked at the *Sunday Times*, the *Daily Telegraph* and the *Independent*, as well as numerous British magazines. She appears as a broadcaster on Radio 4. She is married to the writer Philip Kerr. They have three children and live in London.

MARTIN HONEYSETT

is a renowned cartoonist and illustrator, whose work has appeared in *Punch*, *Private Eye*, the *Evening Standard*, the *Observer*, the *Oldie* and many other magazines and newspapers.